LOVE YOU ETERNALLY

DEEPAK RAWAT

Made with ♥ on the Notion Press Platform
www.notionpress.com

Contents

AGONY

1. Pain   3

2. Hurts   4

3. Enough   5

4. Able   6

5. You   7

6. Immortal   8

7. Chaos   9

8. What Is It?   10

9. Beauty   11

10. Need   12

11. Class   13

12. Deceive   14

13. Unbearable   15

14. I Won't Go   16

15. Goodness Sake   17

16. Anytime   18

17. Special   19

18. Why?   20

19. No One Else   21

20. Elixir   22

21. Omnipresent   23

22. Screams   24

23. Heart Out   25

24. Fantasy   26

25. Good Bye   27

Contents

26. Eternal — 28

27. Everything — 29

28. Saviour — 30

29. Perfect Love — 31

30. Art Of Pain — 32

31. Game — 33

32. Nothing Else — 34

33. Fix Me — 35

34. So Many Times — 36

35. Difference — 37

36. Ways — 38

37. Poesy — 39

38. Last Chance — 40

39. Wilt — 41

40. Hell — 42

41. Scrounger — 43

42. Giving — 44

43. Peace And You — 45

44. Helpless — 46

45. Hobby — 47

46. Hope — 48

47. A Night Like This — 49

48. Stop — 50

49. Us — 51

50. Our Relationship — 52

51. Stray — 53

Contents

52. For You   54

53. Spoken Out   55

54. Sorry   56

55. Incurable   57

RECOVERY

56. Time Heals   61

57. Changes   62

58. Curing   63

59. Healing   64

60. After   65

61. Routine   66

62. Magic   67

63. Love Yourself   68

64. Mend   69

65. After Time   70

66. Can't Choose   71

67. Spring   72

STILL YOURS

68. Home   75

69. Stories   76

70. Your Love   77

71. Shall I?   78

72. Epic   79

73. Dream   80

74. Love   81

75. Chanting   82

Contents

76. Last Breathe 83

77. Heart Attack 84

78. Extreme 85

79. To See You 86

80. You & I 87

81. Quake 88

82. Too Close 89

83. I Can't 90

84. Always Yours 91

85. Our Night 92

86. Still Yours 93

Thank you for picking this little piece of me. This book is a set of emotions I wanted to free from my heart and mind. It's impossible to figure out why you get to bear the pain even after loving someone deeply and immensely. Even though, you go through it chanting on the beads of love. But at last, you have no other option than to heal. But, that's not the end. Healing in love and healing the wounds are not the same. Unloving doesn't exist. You still love.

Dear,

I tried my best even in my worst to prove my love for you (was it necessary?). I don't want your love back, maybe I need it. I just wanted you to feel me. I know it's late and we grew really very apart. But a part of my heart still cries for you. This book is my only hope to let my screams reach your heart and let you make them stop (I wish you would). I went through pain and healing but still, **I LOVE YOU**.

I love you till death and rebirth,

I love you to the moon and back,

I love you up to the count of the stars,

I LOVE YOU ETERNALLY.

AGONY

1. PAIN

• 3 •

Loving you gave me pain
And that pain made me
Love you more.

2. HURTS

I know it hurts
Talking to you
And caring for you
But I can't stop
Because I love you.

3. ENOUGH

• 5 •

You tried your best
To carry the broken pieces
Of my heart,
But they slipped.
They can't take it anymore.

4. ABLE

• 6 •

The pain tells how much you loved.

5. YOU

This agony is killing me
Wounds won't hurt
Death seems luxury
But it's okay
Because it was you.

6. IMMORTAL

For all the pain that
I don't deserve
I have words to cure them
But,
What about the memories?
They won't go,

7. CHAOS

• 9 •

You left my heart in chaos
Noises I can't hear and
The silence is too loud.

8. WHAT IS IT?

What is it if not love?
When they pray for you,
To be with you.
When they bear all the pain,
Even if you don't deserve.
When their soul felt enough,
But they still tried.
What is it if not love?
What is it?

9. BEAUTY

Your love made my words rhyme
The pain made it beautiful.

10. NEED

Is there any word like sympathy in you?
Because I need it,
Before I die for you.

11. CLASS

Love teaches you lessons
But breaking hearts
Is out of the syllabus.

12. DECEIVE

• 14 •

You gave pain to my heart
But my eyes cried
For what they saw was you
Whom they never believed would be.

13. UNBEARABLE

What love is this?
If you have to express it in words.
What pain is this?
If you have no words to show.

14. I WON'T GO

Where do broken hearts go?
To the darkness they say.
Where there is no other soul,
Where they can hear the echo of their
Own screams
Because the aching is real
And it won't go.

15. GOODNESS SAKE

• 17 •

Sleep before the midnight dear,
Tears after 2 AM never dry.

16. ANYTIME

I was ready to be broken by you.
Anytime.
But not now,
No piece of me is left to be more broken.

17. SPECIAL

They say first love is the best feeling
But first heart break is even better,
It makes you love the person more than before.

18. WHY?

You know, how much you
Make my heartthrob
And still, you ask me
Why?
Why do I cry?
Why do I bleed?
Let me give you some burden of my guilt that I loved you,
Even when I should not.
And you dare not
Ask me why?

19. NO ONE ELSE

Loving someone else?
I would prefer losing you again.

20. ELIXIR

When you started feeling for her
Your soul drank the elixir of love
And I swear to you,
Poison won't kill you, dear.

21. OMNIPRESENT

• 23 •

Your love is like the moon
sometimes full
sometimes nothing
mine is like the stars,
the more you search
the more you find.

22. SCREAMS

I have been telling you that
I don't want your love back,
Maybe I've been lying.
This heart screams to be loved.

23. HEART OUT

I don't write for a cause
I write for you.
I write to you.
My love for you fills ink in my pen
And it cries when my heart aches
Then,
It spills out some words
That is my urge to tell you,
How I've been without you.

24. FANTASY

This heart is a desert
Your love is mirage.

25. GOOD BYE

When I breathe my last
Tell her that I loved her.
If she misses me
Ask her to look at the sky
And the brightest star would be me.

26. ETERNAL

You gave me pain
And I loved it.
You gave me more
Now I am addicted to it.
I want to keep myself in pain, forever,
And make it even worse for me.
I won't kill myself
I won't make it so easy.
I will let myself starve for mercy,
I will let myself drown in agony
And swallowed by the darkness.
I will bath in the trauma you rained on me
And make my love ETERNAL

27. EVERYTHING

• 29 •

Life is beautiful
Some say with wealth
Some say with health
I say with you.
How beautiful it may be
But it is worthless
If I don't have you.

28. SAVIOUR

This heart refuses
To beat unless you are
With me
So, could you please save me for this life?
The other I don't need.

29. PERFECT LOVE

• 31 •

My heart is a complete mess

And you are the reason

It cries for your cry,

And also cries when you cry.

Because it knows,

This is not how love works

If the love was not from both sides

Then, why shall be the hate?

30. ART OF PAIN

Love makes you blind
You can't write
But pain makes you an artist
You create masterpiece.

31. GAME

When I think of you
I hardly think of love
Love with you was sweet
But the ache
It makes me feel weak in the bones
My soul shivers in terror
Everything was planned, right?
You keep on hurting
I keep on loving
Was it a game?
Then, sorry I played it wrong.

32. NOTHING ELSE

I only craved
Two things
Either you or death.

33. FIX ME

I hope for the day
When you will
Find me and
Take me home
To fix me.
Don't search for me
Somewhere far
I might be near you.

34. SO MANY TIMES

If I were to plant a tree

For every time

You hurt me.

I would have

Grown a vast

And a dense forest.

You would never

Find me in it.

I would be screeching my heart and tearing my soul

35. DIFFERENCE

Darling,
The stars aren't dim today
Your eyes are filled with tears,
For them, whose nights are
Beautiful like a full moon.

36. WAYS

If there was even a single way
To be with you,
Believe me, I tried.

37. POESY

This poetry
Were once my words
That I used to speak myself
Pretending you were listening.

38. LAST CHANCE

• 40 •

I would have given up already,
But this little heart wants to try once more.

39. WILT

• 41 •

I can't show you my heart
I don't want to scare you.
It's been a terrible place
Ever since you left me to wilt.

40. HELL

• 42

I may not write so well,
Because I write about the pain
And it was never good.

41. SCROUNGER

• 43 •

Love is a climber
It takes all over the heart
Yours was a parasite

42. GIVING

On you,

I showered all the love

I have

I am now left with nothing

But pain and hate

I get it from you and

I give it to me as well.

43. PEACE AND YOU

• 45 •

After all this pain, trauma, panic
And chaos.
I want to air in and breathe out everything
I want a break forever
I want to rest in peace.
But my heart refuses
"There is peace after death, but not you".
It said

44. HELPLESS

I can be the moon you long for,
But you took away the light from me.

45. HOBBY

My favourite pastime,
When I am alone,
Is to subject myself
To abuse.
I run your memories and
Rate them, which one was the
Most painful I ask myself
And then cry myself to sleep.

46. HOPE

• 48 •

I was like a tree in autumn

Which shed all its leaves.

A living dead.

But still rooted.

In a hope of spring to return.

47. A NIGHT LIKE THIS

Last night
When the stars were out
The moon had a peak on
My window.
She saw me crying for you
I looked at her
She looked elsewhere
When I rolled my eyes
She was looking at me
Our eyes met at once.
I saw you in her.
She had tears in her eyes too.
Her hands wept my tears off
I begged her to stay
And she did.
I was the happiest at that moment,
Giggling like a child.
It all ended when I came to know it was a dream
But I had you there
What else would I long for?
I slept in peace.

48. STOP

If this pain is to grew
Any harder,
I won't survive
I am already in the edge of self destruction.
On the roof of a tall building.
I stood
I seem to be firm and well rooted
But even a small wind
Can push me to death.

49. US

When I cry for you,
I cry so loud
I have to put a
Pillow in my mouth,
Still, the cry is so loud that
The windows get open
And the walls yell at me
To stop.
But knowing only you can make this stop.
They pray for us.

50. OUR RELATIONSHIP

It wasn't going anywhere
So, I carried.

51. STRAY

When you left
It took some time for
My heart to shatter
First of all, I felt homeless.

52. FOR YOU

No one would like to cry
But, if the reason of my tears are you
I would forget the reason
To smile.

53. SPOKEN OUT

• 55 •

"Peace and death are synonyms to each"
The smallest piece of a broken heart said

54. SORRY

It was me who prayed for your happiness
But, sometimes it hurts
When I see you happy.
Sometimes your smile stab my heart
And the blood flow through my eyes.
I can't see you so happy
After the way you treated me.
This world is a cruel place
You showed me more of it,
With that smile on your face
And no sympathy in your stoned heart.

55. INCURABLE

The disease of love
Has no cure
The symptoms are you
Cry at night and
Bleed in the day
You will die for sure
But, slowly- slowly.
Very slowly.

RECOVERY

56. TIME HEALS

• 61 •

Dear self,
Have patience.
It takes time for
Time to heal.

57. CHANGES

This little heart can't take it anymore
Tired of pain
And feared of love
It wants to come out
It wants to heal and wants to mend
It wants to beat again
But this time for me.

58. CURING

I found a piece of me missing
After you
After a long time, I smiled,
Looking in my mirror.
After a very long time.
It smiled back

59. HEALING

• 64 •

I something bad is to happen
I smile.
I don't get scared
As I know, nothing can
Be worse than what
You did to me.

60. AFTER

Once I run out of tears
I would look at the stars
That looked so dim and blur,
These many days.
I would not be searching for you
I'd rather breathe you out.

61. ROUTINE

Joy and sorrow
Resembles the sun
And the moon
One set and the other rises.

62. MAGIC

Time talks to the
Wounds in a way
That they heal so beautifully.
I wonder what it says.

63. LOVE YOURSELF

Why beg for love?
When you can give
It to yourself
The purest and the kindest of all.

64. MEND

But darling,
The moon still shines
Whether the stars show up or not.

65. AFTER TIME

After some time
Your eyes won't cry
Your heart won't ache
This pain is temporary.
You can heal and shine
And the after is always beautiful.

66. CAN'T CHOOSE

• 71 •

Letting go is not easy
Holding on is even harder.

67. SPRING

Oh, dear!
I know you are bleeding
I can see
You are crying too.
I also know you hurt yourself
To distract your heart.
But
Please stop
Don't ruin the best of you.
Just heal.
Try.
Let the spring come

STILL YOURS

68. HOME

• 75 •

I could have been anywhere
But I wanted to be in your feet

69. STORIES

Your eyes continues
When your lips stop talking.

70. YOUR LOVE

The moon gives you her lap
The stars sing you a lullaby
Sun won't rise till you wake up
Because,
You my love are what
They are made for.

71. SHALL I?

Shall I fetch all
The star for you?
To show that even they
Love you too.
Or is it enough that
I tell you and I do.
Shall I ask the
Moon to take rest?
For I have you to brighten my life.

72. EPIC

The sun is forever
The moon is forever
My love for you is also forever
Then what is stopping you and me
From becoming us.
Are the stars at fault?
Don't worry I told the sky about them.
Let's unify again and give this whole
Universe an epic of great love.

73. DREAM

• 80 •

A fairy with a pen
In its hand
Wrote about me and you
I was the poem of love
And you were the love in it.

74. LOVE

Sometimes I hold you
Tighter,
Not to hurt you
But to tell you that
I love you, and I
Declare this holding
The language of my love.

75. CHANTING

People sigh
I take your name.

76. LAST BREATHE

In complete darkness,
Where we barely see ourselves.
I hope I could find your arm
And crawl near it.
Curl myself and rest my head
On it.
I hope the screams
In me would stop then.
I would take a deep breathe.
My last breathe.

77. HEART ATTACK

• 84 •

Every time your lips
Touch mine, I have
To warn my heart
140 beats per minute is normal.

78. EXTREME

I hate the way I love you too much.

79. TO SEE YOU

Sun and moon
Fight each other
Every day.
The reason is you
The sun sets the moon to see you
And the moon does the same.

80. YOU & I

Darling,
Our love is not something
Which can be written or told.
But something, for which
The flowers bloom and
The trees grow,
Something for which
Galaxies merge and
The stars twinkle.
Something for which
People dance and
Music happens.

81. QUAKE

When your eyes
Meet mine, my legs
Tremble so hard it causes
A quake in my heart.

82. TOO CLOSE

• 89 •

Bring me close to you,
Let not your heartbeat
Sleep me.

83. I CAN'T

They say loving ourselves is
The best way to heal.
But forgetting you
Is like deceiving myself.
My heart won't take it.

84. ALWAYS YOURS

Come back
Even as a dream,
Even as a pain,
In any form
In any way
I am all yours.

85. OUR NIGHT

We are under the same roof.
The sky.
Surrounded by the stars.
The moon looking at us.
Look at her.
Smile.
That's it.
All night is ours now.

86. STILL YOURS

I loved you as if
I was born for it.
I tried everything possible to make
You realize what I feel.
I feel that we have a strong bond
Between us.
A bond pure of all means.
But still,
I lost you.
This poetry watered with my tears
Burdened in my pain
Drowning in my blood
And hidden in my trauma
Is my only hope to make you feel
The same.
To make you feel for me.

Thank you so much. You made it till here. I love you. I am blessed that you have been the person who I wished would listen to me with this much patience and love.

All this poetry may or may not be the best to hear but I am sure they were best to relate to.

We all have our ways to love. We have our ways to celebrate it. Some of us may show love in words and others might express it through things they do. but somewhere I believe that we all go through the same pain and hurt.

That's the worst phase of our life. But they all are warriors who survived that. I adore you. I can relate to you I have been there once and it's like I will be there forever. That's what makes your love eternal. Let your pain out and asking for your love is useless. I swear, don't try it at all, You only hurt yourself.

Believe in yourself and you can do miracles. I am not at all suggesting or requesting you forget the person you loved. You can't do that. Unloving is a folk you and I are unfamiliar with until we need it.

Let your love live long.

Let your pain live.

Let yourself rise and never fall again.

Love again.